# CURSIVE
## HANDWRITING
### Word Family Practice Workbook

100+
Reward
Stickers

D1607096

*This book belongs to*

Jam

Wonder House

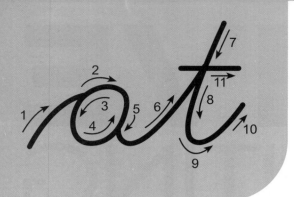

*cat*

## Trace and write

*at          at          at          at*

*bat          bat          bat          bat*

*cat          cat          cat          cat*

*fat          fat          fat          fat*

*hat          hat          hat          hat*

*mat          mat          mat          mat*

*rat          rat          rat          rat*

*that          that          that          that*

Reward          ☆ ☆ ☆

*jam*

Trace and write

am    am    am    am

dam    dam    dam    dam

ham    ham    ham    ham

jam    jam    jam    jam

ram    ram    ram    ram

yam    yam    yam    yam

clam    clam    clam    clam

spam    spam    spam    spam

Reward

crab

## Trace and write

ab    ab    ab    ab

cab    cab    cab    cab

gab    gab    gab    gab

lab    lab    lab    lab

tab    tab    tab    tab

crab    crab    crab    crab

flab    flab    flab    flab

grab    grab    grab    grab

*dad*

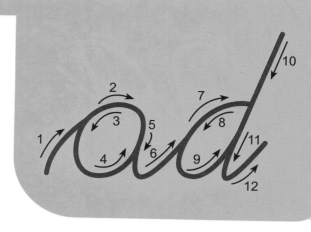

## Trace and write

ad ad ad ad

bad bad bad bad

dad dad dad dad

had had had had

lad lad lad lad

mad mad mad mad

sad sad sad sad

glad glad glad glad

Reward

5

## Trace and write

ag    ag    ag    ag

bag    bag    bag    bag

tag    tag    tag    tag

wag    wag    wag    wag

brag    brag    brag    brag

drag    drag    drag    drag

flag    flag    flag    flag

stag    stag    stag    stag

Reward ☆ ☆ ☆

*cap*

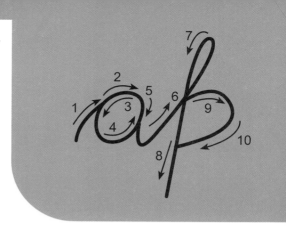

Trace and write

ap    ap    ap    ap

cap    cap    cap    cap

gap    gap    gap    gap

lap    lap    lap    lap

map    map    map    map

tap    tap    tap    tap

clap    clap    clap    clap

slap    slap    slap    slap

Reward

⭐ ⭐ ⭐

7

## Trace and write

an    an    an    an

an    an    an    an

fan    fan    fan    fan

man    man    man    man

pan    pan    pan    pan

van    van    van    van

clan    clan    clan    clan

plan    plan    plan    plan

Reward                    ☆ ☆ ☆

*car*

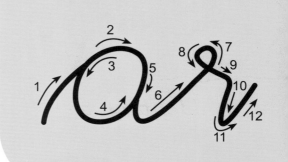

Trace and write

*ar*     *ar*     *ar*     *ar*

*bar*     *bar*     *bar*     *bar*

*car*     *car*     *car*     *car*

*far*     *far*     *far*     *far*

*jar*     *jar*     *jar*     *jar*

*tar*     *tar*     *tar*     *tar*

*scar*     *scar*     *scar*     *scar*

*star*     *star*     *star*     *star*

Reward

9

# Word Family

Identify the pictures and place the words in their word family.

*am*

1. _ _ _ _ _ _ _ _ _ _ _ _ _ _ _ _ _ _ _

2. _ _ _ _ _ _ _ _ _ _ _ _ _ _ _ _ _ _ _

3. _ _ _ _ _ _ _ _ _ _ _ _ _ _ _ _ _ _ _

*at*

1. _ _ _ _ _ _ _ _ _ _ _ _ _ _ _ _ _ _ _

2. _ _ _ _ _ _ _ _ _ _ _ _ _ _ _ _ _ _ _

3. _ _ _ _ _ _ _ _ _ _ _ _ _ _ _ _ _ _ _

 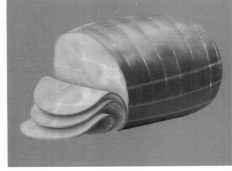 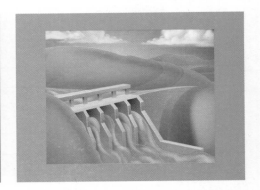

*Reward*

10

# Jumbled Words

Identify the pictures and unscramble the words.

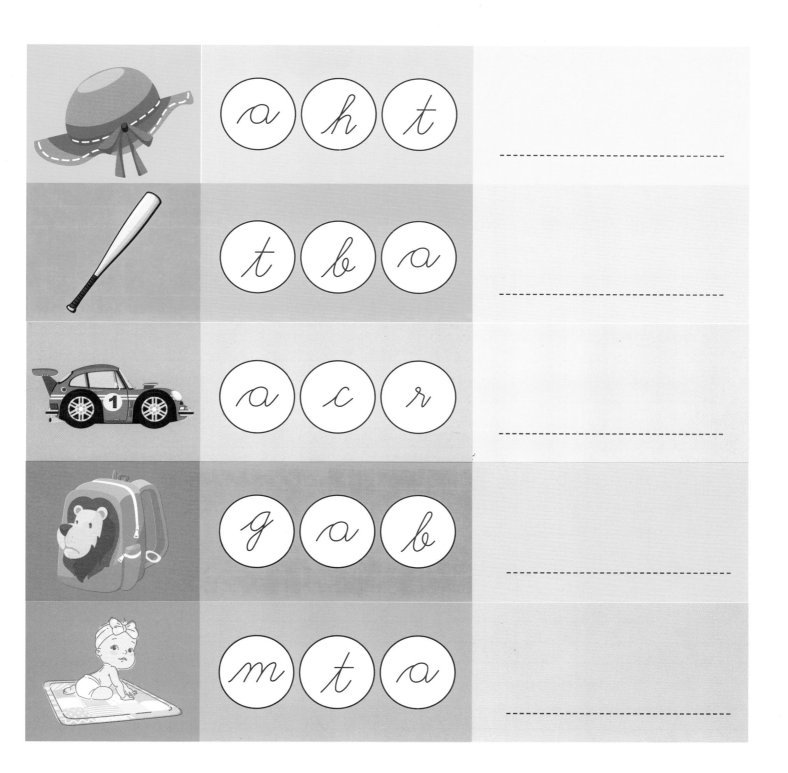

| | a h t | ---------------------------------- |
| | t b a | ---------------------------------- |
| | a c r | ---------------------------------- |
| | g a b | ---------------------------------- |
| | m t a | ---------------------------------- |

Reward

## Trace and write

ee        ee        ee        ee

bee       bee       bee       bee

fee       fee       fee       fee

see       see       see       see

free      free      free      free

glee      glee      glee      glee

knee      knee      knee      knee

tree      tree      tree      tree

Reward

*hen*

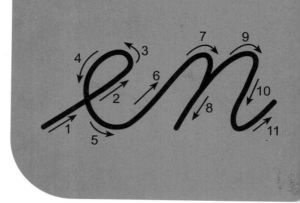

Trace and write

en en en en

den den den den

hen hen hen hen

men men men men

pen pen pen pen

ten ten ten ten

then then then then

when when when when

Reward

☆ ☆ ☆

13

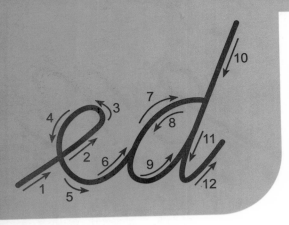

*bed*

## Trace and write

ed          ed          ed          ed

bed         bed         bed         bed

fed         fed         fed         fed

led         led         led         led

red         red         red         red

wed         wed         wed         wed

fled        fled        fled        fled

shed        shed        shed        shed

Reward

14

*jet*

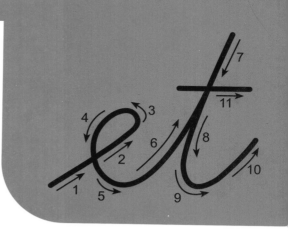

Trace and write

*et  et  et  et*

*jet  jet  jet  jet*

*pet  pet  pet  pet*

*set  set  set  set*

*net  net  net  net*

*wet  wet  wet  wet*

*fret  fret  fret  fret*

*poet  poet  poet  poet*

Reward

*ship*

## Trace and write

ip     ip     ip     ip

dip    dip    dip    dip

hip    hip    hip    hip

rip    rip    rip    rip

sip    sip    sip    sip

tip    tip    tip    tip

flip   flip   flip   flip

slip   slip   slip   slip

*kid*

Trace and write

id     id     id     id

bid     bid     bid     bid

did     did     did     did

hid     hid     hid     hid

kid     kid     kid     kid

lid     lid     lid     lid

mid     mid     mid     mid

rid     rid     rid     rid

Reward

5 ↗   7 ↗

1 →   2 ↓   4 →   8 ↓

3 ↓   6 ↓   9 ↗

*bin*

## Trace and write

*in*    *in*    *in*    *in*

*bin*    *bin*    *bin*    *bin*

*fin*    *fin*    *fin*    *fin*

*pin*    *pin*    *pin*    *pin*

*tin*    *tin*    *tin*    *tin*

*win*    *win*    *win*    *win*

*chin*    *chin*    *chin*    *chin*

*thin*    *thin*    *thin*    *thin*

Reward    ☆ ☆ ☆

*kit*

Trace and write

it    it    it    it

bit    bit    bit    bit

kit    kit    kit    kit

pit    pit    pit    pit

sit    sit    sit    sit

writ    writ    writ    writ

chit    chit    chit    chit

slit    slit    slit    slit

Reward

19

# Word Family

Identify the pictures and place the words in their word family.

1. _____

2. _____

3. _____

1. _____

2. _____

3. _____

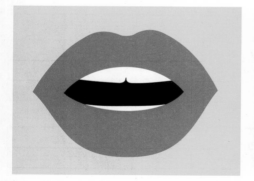

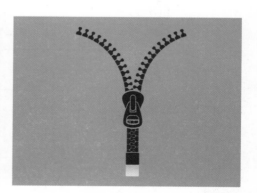

Reward

# Jumbled Words

Identify the pictures and unscramble the words.

| 10 | e  n  t | ------------------------- |
| --- | --- | --- |
| | i  p  n | ------------------------- |
| | s  t  i | ------------------------- |
| | i  n  t | ------------------------- |
| | e  d  r | ------------------------- |

Reward

☆ ☆ ☆

fig

## Trace and write

ig          ig          ig          ig

big         big         big         big

dig         dig         dig         dig

fig         fig         fig         fig

pig         pig         pig         pig

wing        wing        wing        wing

sing        sing        sing        sing

twig        twig        twig        twig

Reward

*knob*

Trace and write

ob      ob      ob      ob

bob      bob      bob      bob

mob      mob      mob      mob

rob      rob      rob      rob

sob      sob      sob      sob

job      job      job      job

knob      knob      knob      knob

slob      slob      slob      slob

Reward

*cop*

## Trace and write

op    op    op    op

cop    cop    cop    cop

hop    hop    hop    hop

mop    mop    mop    mop

pop    pop    pop    pop

top    top    top    top

chop    chop    chop    chop

shop    shop    shop    shop

Reward

*dog*

Trace and write

og    og    og    og

bog    bog    bog    bog

dog    dog    dog    dog

fog    fog    fog    fog

jog    jog    jog    jog

log    log    log    log

clog    clog    clog    clog

frog    frog    frog    frog

Reward

25

*pot*

## Trace and write

ot    ot    ot    ot

bat    bat    bat    bat

cot    cot    cot    cot

dot    dot    dot    dot

got    got    got    got

hot    hot    hot    hot

clot    clot    clot    clot

plot    plot    plot    plot

Reward

*tub*

Trace and write

| ub | ub | ub | ub |

| cub | cub | cub | cub |

| hub | hub | hub | hub |

| rub | rub | rub | rub |

| sub | sub | sub | sub |

| tub | tub | tub | tub |

| club | club | club | club |

| snub | snub | snub | snub |

Reward

⭐ ⭐ ⭐

## Trace and write

*un*       *un*       *un*       *un*

*bun*      *bun*      *bun*      *bun*

*fun*      *fun*      *fun*      *fun*

*pun*      *pun*      *pun*      *pun*

*run*      *run*      *run*      *run*

*sun*      *sun*      *sun*      *sun*

*shun*      *shun*      *shun*      *shun*

*stun*      *stun*      *stun*      *stun*

Reward

*hut*

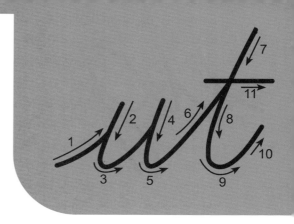

Trace and write

ut    ut    ut    ut

but    but    but    but

cut    cut    cut    cut

gut    gut    gut    gut

hut    hut    hut    hut

rut    rut    rut    rut

glut    glut    glut    glut

shut    shut    shut    shut

Reward

## Trace and write

ug ug ug ug

bug bug bug bug

dug dug dug dug

hug hug hug hug

rug rug rug rug

tug tug tug tug

plug plug plug plug

slug slug slug slug

Reward

*drum*

## Trace and write

sum sum sum sum

gum gum gum gum

hum hum hum hum

mum mum mum mum

sum sum sum sum

drum drum drum drum

plum plum plum plum

slum slum slum slum

Reward